PRAISE FOR JOYCE FUTA'S *LIT WINDOWS*

Joyce Futa is a dreamer in the most real sense. She looks with subtlety at the details, awake or asleep, and writes with a quiet power that will inspire her readers to examine and see themselves in their past and present in new ways. Tanka prose and haibun seem her natural voice. Each piece is indeed a "lit window", into which we look in quietly and watch her dream world unfold, her everyday life, her memories, where each object has significance and emotional and literary power. For her, as on her collection of Japanese plates, Mt. Fuji is always in the distance. She muses about her uncle:

> "Japanese American
> struggles within
> the ancient armor"

Her natural talent for these Japanese forms seems personal and her insights have a unique perspective. Any object she holds is imbued with meaning, just as we feel in our dreams. They are important, symbolic but mysterious. Her writing, just as the bamboo basket she describes:

"turns and folds around thrusting sticks with curves and indentations of a natural life.

> it holds something
> an onion, blue beads
> a bright meditation"

Sometimes we don't know if she has invited us into a dream world, her life as it was, or is now. But always we see her moving and our own reflections in her inviting and insightful "Lit Windows". Her beautiful book holds treasures you will want to pick up and reflect upon, again and again.

—Kath Abela Wilson, Secretary, Tanka Society of America

Joyce Futa casts time into long waves of elegant prose, and then gathers what remains in her poet's net, finding "red jewels [that] glisten/ among membranes/ of memory." With deep noticing, tenderness, and wit, she measures the ways we are shaped and reshaped by everyone who moves through our lives, even through our dreams. This book is a record of "looking up at stars/ through bare branches," tracing the light that comes when one distance touches another.

—Brent Armendinger, Author of *The Ghost in Us Was Multiplying*

Joyce Futa's *Lit Windows* builds with a quiet intensity, much like a great soup whose signature dish is tasted as much through the mystery of its chef as its individual ingredients. And taste we do, *slippery as seaweed in broth, with a crisp maple leaf floating on top. We inhale[d] the sweet steam, remembering when all the colors had drifted down in a slow spiral of air.* This spiral reaches our senses and functions not as a collection of poems but a memoir of dream and memory, alive with persons and place and beautifully crafted into haunting, profound and sometimes humorous haibuns. A perfect form to capture life's ephemera. Yet, while a number of Futa's haibuns seem autobiographical, they are never merely personal. *Lit Windows* asks us to reflect on the culture of family whether in the context of Futa's Japanese-American upbringing or our own splintered roots. It is also a history of displacement where immigrants come to a strange and unwelcoming land and try to find their way toward a sense of belonging. But the palette extends outward to the philosophical as *Lit Windows* takes on the spectrum of beginnings and endings casting our loves and our losses into nourishment of the soul. Here, wisdom sits not with pretention but in the skilled measure of one called upon to observe both our bright and fading worlds.

—Lois P. Jones, Poetry Editor, *Kyoto Journal*

LIT WINDOWS:

A BOOK OF HAIBUN AND TANKA PROSE

by

Joyce Futa

BLUE LIGHT PRESS ◆ 1ST WORLD PUBLISHING

1ST WORLD
PUBLISHING

SAN FRANCISCO ◆ FAIRFIELD ◆ DELHI

LIT WINDOWS:
A BOOK OF HAIBUN AND TANKA PROSE

Copyright ©2017 by Joyce Futa

1ST WORLD LIBRARY
PO Box 2211
Fairfield, IA 52556
www.1stworldpublishing.com

BLUE LIGHT PRESS
www.bluelightpress.com
Email: bluelightpress@aol.com

BOOK & COVER DESIGN
Melanie Gendron
www.melaniegendron.com

COVER ART
"Sonetto in Morte di Madonna Laura" by Toti O'Brien

AUTHOR PHOTOGRAPH
Liz Goetz

FIRST EDITION

ISBN: 978-1-4218-3772-7

Acknowledgment

Many thanks to my poetry teachers Brent Armendinger, Mary De-Nardo, Kathabela Wilson, and Diane Frank for their inspiration, encouragement, and for instilling in me an appreciation for the fine art of crafting a poem.

Previously Published

Previous versions of following poems were published in the following anthologies or journals:

"Driving to LA on 5", "The Dining Table", "Animus", and "Poston, AZ, 1985" in *I Saw My Ex at a Party*, anthology of the 2008 Intergenerational Writing Lab, Kearny Street Workshop and Intersection for the Arts, San Francisco.

"Sky" and "Animus" in *Bright Stars, An Organic Tanka Anthology*, publiished by KeiBooks, 2011.

"Painting of Woman, Poston, AZ, 1942" and "Jacks" in *Drawn to the Light*, 2015 Southern California Haiku Study Group Anthology.

"Spirit Horse" in *Wind Can't Touch*, 2016 Southern California Haiku Study Group Anthology.

LIT WINDOWS:

A BOOK OF HAIBUN AND TANKA PROSE

TABLE OF CONTENTS

SYNCHRONICITY

I dreamt I was in San Francisco again, looking out the bay window at the apartment across the street where we once lived, where our friends now live. I thought how nice to be back and to be in Altadena, the best of two possible worlds.

You came in, my husband — which one were you? — Don, maybe John? Utterly pleasant, without the old tension, you said "I want some Indian pizza" — which was exactly what I wanted. You offered to go down to the corner and get some, which made me even happier.

The kids were sleeping in the back bedroom, and the ghost cat snuggled next to our new dog.

I thought how perfect everything is. We were young, and no less wise than we are now.

        split open
        pomegranate
        red jewels glisten
        among membranes
        of memory

Leaving SF: An Allegory

Last night, you told me you were marrying my old love John whom I hadn't seen in years except in dreams. I had gone to his house to pick up a few things and you were there. *Mysterious*, I thought.

I talked to John and touched him in the old ways while you watched, and felt intense bonds between us all in that small familiar room. Finally I understood. You looked at me and nodded.

Plans for your new life were dancing in your eyes. You showed me photos of the mansion you were renovating to accommodate his wheelchair. I was astounded by your wealth.

I cried, *I didn't know — when, where did you meet?* You said, *Here, you were here when it all began*, and I realized it was true. Birds in my head had chattered when I went away, half knowing it was over. You said you wanted me to know. We were warm, tearful. I saw how it was good.

I put some receipts and photos into my wallet and prepared to leave.

> rooms in the city
> where I lived
> still lit

ALTADENA SOUP

It seemed that someone had made a soup of all the leaves on the ground, and we were amazed at its goodness. It was slippery as seaweed in broth, with a crisp maple leaf floating on top. We inhaled the sweet steam, remembering when all the colors had drifted down in a slow spiral of air.

Now, in the bowl was a tidepool of surprises — soft spongy birchbark, snippets of fern, and tiny bright mums.

Each flavor and texture reminded us of childhood, aunties cooking and laughing together, golden afternoons of nothing but play, when everything new was in the air and blowing our way.

       clopping on imagined horses
       ranch of a vacant lot
       busy children
       canter to a stop
       high noon of lunch

JACKS

When we played, life was orderly, rhythmic. One could begin to see the path to mastery: practice, concentration, intense quiet competition. The jacks felt like heavy sparks in our hands before we threw them. We loved the ringing clatter and hiss as they fell and skidded into formation. The bouncing ball set time and rhythm to picking up the jacks, one by one, two by two — until one swept them all into the palm and caught the ball.

Like rival ballerinas we studied each other's hands, the poise of the fingers, the curve and sweep of the palm, but it was my cousin's fat little hand that made the most amazing moves. We sat on the floor and played and played, the variations getting more complex, the ball bouncing, the jacks singing, a childhood afternoon passing.

> hocus pocus
> cast a spell
> a spray of stars

IMMIGRANTS

We wrote many letters to each other, from California to Japan, Japan to California, before I promised your grandfather to leave my family and marry him. Yet from the beginning I knew. Something in him was in me too, a desire to leave confines and grow into a stronger self.

In the beginning it was very hard, working the farm in the hot desert. Fine sand drifted into our rooms with slow air. Homesick, I wept. I couldn't bear the place, the unfriendly people. Finally, he said you may go back, but you must leave the child. So I did not speak of that again and took my place beside him.

We worked very hard and began to prosper. Pearl Harbor happened and the camps, where we tried not to think that what we had gained might all be lost.

But you were born there, my first grandchild. I felt such joy holding you, hummed Japanese songs, played peek-a-boo. I wonder what you will remember of me. I follow you with outstretched hands as you begin to walk into your world.

> barren desert
> the old couple exclaim —
> peach girl!

Mt. Fuji from a Distance

To imagine my grandmother's time and place, I collect painted Japanese plates where women in kimonos wander in spring by a lake or river, joyful in each other's company. They talk, point, dance, sing. Willows drift in a soft breeze, maybe a turtle is sunning on a log. Mt. Fuji is always in the distance.

Such sweet respite from their lives of washing rice, pounding cloths, scurrying small-stepped toward the call of men. I used to think it was my father's innate nature, darkly imperious, that ruled with blind ignorance our caught family. Only later did I understand it was also the myth of strong men and that he would not withstand his daughters growing up.

> and now I drift
> green path by lake
> feeling almost free

Painting of Woman, Poston, AZ, 1942

("The Evacuee" by Tokio Ueyama)

She reminds me of my mother, for she too was pregnant in 1942. She too was confined to barracks in the middle of the desert, where purple mountains spoke obstacle, bright stars at night spoke insignificance.

In this moment, the woman seems content, sitting in a chair in the barracks, knitting some small white thing. Her hair is rolled and tucked around her head, her blouse and skirt loose, one leg draped over the other. Thin curtains are on the windows, a large thermos jug on the planked floor, a pair of sandals askew against the wall. The door is wide open to the desert, and the light is beautiful. She is enjoying a moment of solitude in that densely peopled life — families crowded into barracks, huge mess halls, unprivate bath houses. Through the curtains one sees rows and rows of barracks, perspective making the identical smaller and smaller, but no one else is visible.

She reminds me of my mother, for she was young and beautiful then too. Although I left the internment camp when I was three, I remember it like a dream landscape: the desert light, hot dry air, immense sky, raw wood walls. My mother would rarely speak of that time. But later, amidst the clamor of her children, she would now and then draw into herself and stare into the afternoon.

> after the war
> mowing green
> southern California lawns
> Japanese gardeners
> remembered the desert

THE DINING TABLE

Father and I sat on one side of the table, little brother and sister on the narrow end, mother went back and forth to the kitchen, then sat with my other sister facing us. Every night of my childhood, we sat in formation with minimal talk, passing spaghetti, sashimi, fried chicken, tempura, burgers, or tofu, and always rice.

I hated these meals, picked at the food, shoved unwanted piles off to the side, making walls. I fantasized a different family, one without my stern father who wasn't comfortable speaking English and ate displeased in critical silence. We all didn't talk much except for little remarks from my hopeful mother passing food around, or from my sister Amy, who always tried to be normal.

At big family gatherings when my grandfather, aunts and uncles were there, my father spoke in Japanese, became expansive, witty, entertained the company. *Phony!* I thought, getting up from the table. But even then, what I didn't know, what I would never know about my father, made me pause in my anger and stumble.

> at their graves
> we divide flowers evenly
> between mother and father

SISTERS

We thought about clothes and dreamt about nakedness. Jealous, we fought and wept; the borrowed sweater ended up on the floor. My mother entered the room and hissed. She could hardly wait for us to grow up.

Feral cats prowled the neighborhood, pouncing upon their little kills, dipping into starry water.

The days were long. We snapped at each other until we finally lay down to sleep. In that small moonlit bedroom, forgiveness was only a dream.

>we have grown old
>the world small again
>blood ties
>no matter what
>we tell each other

Not Quite

Some fingers fly as nimble as bees, taking tiny hand stiches, guiding fabric through a machine like magic. My mother's were painstaking, undoing, redoing seam after seam. Through the years, she pinned and basted, fitted and refitted dozens of dresses as we stood on the table so she could see it wasn't quite right.

We sighed, we slumped, we turned around as my mother muttered, her mouth full of pins. "Stand straight," she said through careful tight lips, aligning the hem somewhere along our skinny bowlegs.

We didn't get to choose the fabric, and the dress didn't look like it came from a store. It wasn't quite what everyone was wearing, although when finished, it fit perfectly.

> careless children
> clothes on the floor
> now we fold
> not quite
> wrinkle-free

THINGS WE WILL NEVER KNOW

Lost in some dream that circled her life, my mother sat at the kitchen table with a steaming cup of coffee. We knew better than to ask what she was thinking. It would have been, *"Nothing, go play."*

Out parents rarely talked about themselves. At family gatherings, our ears perked up; we always learned something we didn't know. My aunt said, *"Your mother was so quiet. I was the one who was always yakking. Pop said he wished he could even us out."*

My uncle said, *"Your father, oldest son, was spoiled. He was always first, took the best, expected it."* Two solitary Japanese gardeners.

We poured over family photos, my mother submissive and beautiful, my father dark and imperious. *What a mismatch!* we came to think.

> her silence
> and his
> then I became
> caught
> in my own secrets

The Teenage Poet

She reads haikus and Emily Dickinson, amazed how words proceed in a line, then turn and open into something else. She writes herself, rambling through moods, staring up at disappointing skies, enters a contest and wins third prize.

She paints her nails, talks on the phone to friends, leans into the mirror to put on blue eye shadow. Vamping at a mirror, she searches for simile: "I look like a parakeet."

Once in a while, a line comes to mind that she knows is good. She rolls it into a curler, until it sets, ready to spring.

> her parents know
> there is a mind there
> but it will be a while

PROMENADE

I had written a letter to my first great love, my high school algebra teacher, telling him finally how it was with me. I was truthful and eloquent; it was beautifully crafted, and as I walked along the promenade where I was likely to see him after all these years, among so many faces, I fretted. Did I send that letter? Or did I dream I sent that letter?

I sent my son, a boy again, away on an errand because I felt I would see him. And there he was, glad to see me. He had gotten my letter, clasped my hand and looked into my eyes. I saw he was standing on a stool, that he was a little person, and I wondered... Can I still love him?

Then in an instant, he turned into five men, each slightly different, and we wandered through vast ancient rooms to a balcony overlooking the sea, where marble ruins circled the harbor.

As we sipped our drinks, I held forth with scant knowledge on the promenade's archaeology, and the five men, each with one fifth the intellect of my first great love, listened to me, fascinated.

> high school
> so painful
> to meet your eyes
> I tried to meet
> your expectations

Poston, Arizona, 1985

After we left in 1945, the Indians came to upgrade their housing. The empty barracks were better than what they had.

We rode on buses from Laughlin's casinos to this place in the desert where it seemed there was nothing. Our leader on the bus speaker joked, remembering toilets without doors, trays and trays of pork and beans, and that damned daily apple butter. Some nodded their heads and chuckled.

We were returning to dedicate a memorial, a granite pillar rising into the sky, to remember the past, never forget, and celebrate success against odds. Some dressed in expensive suits and dresses, stood with Congressional aides who read smooth congratulations. Most of us were in comfortable clothes. Many chose not to come.

The Indians were there too, in solidarity, the practical ones, not the young and angry. It was a chance to supplement their government checks by providing a lunch of fry bread and stew, dished out under tents to polite Japanese who silently compared parallel fates.

A few older Indian women performed for us, shifting their weight from foot to foot, chanting songs to a solemn drum.

>   the harm so great
>   centuries have passed
>   slow desert sun

THE GERMAN BOY

When I was nineteen in the early sixties, finally away from home and lost, I lived in the Castro with three other girls in a tiny apartment up on a hill. A beautiful German boy drifted into our lives, living nowhere, anywhere.

He sat on our sofa and listened to jazz, letting cigarette ashes fall to the floor, not to be rude, but in love with disorder.

After the war, his Nazi father could not make him march, took him to a shrink who said he had the mind of an assassin, which horrified his gentle heart.

We went to Golden Gate Park one night, lovelier, he said, than during the day. In white light and shadows, for there was a moon, we sat under trees in a little glen. "Look up and around! The air is so fragrant! Listen!" I did for a minute, then asked to leave, ill at ease with the park and his rapturous spirit in the silvery night.

Who is he now? A musician, professor, a father perhaps? Or did he continue on that path of youth, veering away from all that was cruel? Once in a while on my morning walks, I see a man wrapped in blankets sleeping on a bluff overlooking the ocean. From the near distance of time, I say to the boy:

> you live amidst beauty
> and listen alone
> to the rolling symphonies of night

Puerto Barrios, Guatemala, 1977

We had been warned it was a very rough town, but we had to stay for the next day's ferry. We locked ourselves into a dingy room and waited till morning, when the sailors had passed out and beaten prostitutes slept.

At the ferry station I met the gaze of a young man, soft dark eyes in a quiet face. We spoke very slow Spanish across the few feet between us. He said he had been at sea for years, never earning enough to go back home. It was his fate; where was I from?

He was so beautiful, my friend Anita stepped out from the background to flirt with him. But he kept looking at me in that sunlit room, and I stood very still. I knew he was remembering half a world away, across vast, unrelenting seas, someone very much like me.

> endless ocean
> day and night skies
> I see him
> ship of lost hope
> sailing

Point Reyes

I used to walk those trails above the ocean almost every Sunday with
Maggie and Anita, sometimes with John and others, all of whom I
lost to diverging lives. Trails circled the hills, hawks wheeled in the
sky, rabbits and quail quickly crossed our path as we talked and circled
the drama of our lives.

Looking out as far as we could see, over fields of wild mustard in the
sun's hot brilliance, we anticipated lake, waterfall, beach, and the great
washing ocean, where we would sit on rocks, devour our sandwiches,
then settle into not talking at all. We listened to gulls and the roll of
the ocean, watched wave after wave, pelicans gliding, till we roused
ourselves from the deep vast wild and packed up to go home.

Albino deer grazed on the hillside, gleaming like ghosts in the rosy
twilight. We knew that they would amaze us again in our blessed lives
of those years.

> our youth somehow
> we kept it together
> sacred Sundays
> out of small apartments
> into blue air

At Ocean Beach

When I drove into the parking lot, he waved me to a stop like a cop. He was about my age, stern, strange, white, a little dirty. He signaled me to roll down my window. I fumbled for the door lock button without looking down and hit the window button instead. It rolled down. He glanced at me briefly, then away.

He looked angry, hopeless (*just my luck*, he seemed to think), sighed and asked, "Do you speak English?"

"Yes I do," I replied.

He said, looking even farther away, "Can you help me?"

I said "No, I'm very sorry I cannot."

He stepped back like a cop, waved me on, and I drove away, remembering.

> it had been a while
> I'd almost forgotten
> how some people saw me
> before I could be
> myself

UNCLE TOM

I didn't quite like him, he was so boisterous. "Put up your dukes!" he'd say to my little brother. I'd creep out of his presence whenever I could, but my sister could handle him. "Little Iodine" he'd call her in affectionate kinship, and she'd grin like a shiny new penny.

Now in the hospital, older than anyone dreamed he would be, he gripped my hand strongly as ever, thanked me for coming, and wept. "He's very emotional" said my cousin Bill, and as we talked, Uncle Tom closed his eyes, listened, and wavered on the edge of sleep as things were adjusted, emptied and filled.

He was not the man I remembered, but maybe that was not who he was. Under my father's stern gaze, his younger brother spun with bravado, laughed, drank, and played, the world bright and treacherous. Maybe he was always very emotional.

> Japanese American
> struggles within
> the ancient armor

Two Japanese Bamboo Baskets

Paring the bamboo, aged and smoked, into exact strips, the master creates the perfect abstract of many windows in air curving like earth in space. Fine complex plaits, like metal folded and pulled, edge the rims and up the sides into the arc of the handle. Yet detail is subservient to open delicate suspension.

A different master uses bolder strips to create a form with an aberration, like a large burnished scar emerging from old flesh. It turns and folds around thrusting sticks with the curves and indentations of a natural life.

> it holds something
> an onion, blue beads,
> a bright meditation

INTO GREAT SILENCE

(After the 2007 documentary by Philip Groning)

In a mountain monastery monks in separate places perform tasks in solitude...prepare beds for planting as snow drifts down... pray, read, chop carrots and onions for the soup each will eat alone in his cell... pray, sweep, look out white windows with an inner eye.

They wake at dawn, the track of their days like grooves, attention solely on task and prayer. Silence accrues in snow, rain, and sun.

Some have faces one could imagine on city men walking downtown. How have they come to seek this devotion, paring life down to a clean space for the great silence of prayer?

> ordinary mysteries
> silent repetitions
> prayer infuses
> plowing the field
> slicing the carrot

Enchanted Cottage

I once lived across the street from a little girl named Ruth and her grandmother Leah. They lived on the hill in a pale green cottage, surrounded by a profusion of blue and white cineraria. The house seemed to float, aloft in blossoms. Ruth had been adopted by Leah's daughter and husband, who weren't able to love the child enough. One day she asked her grandmother if she could live with her, and things became instantly and permanently right.

Soon after I moved to the neighborhood, they invited me over for dinner. Ruth took me upstairs and handed me her big old-fashioned doll with a face as round and serious as her own. I felt like I was holding a live infant. Then she showed me the back yard, her rabbit in a hutch, and picked a big raspberry for me to taste. Leah bustled here and there, prepared a lovely salad and pasta from her garden veggies, and we ate, talked, and laughed into the soft summer evening.

> silvered
> we are all
> children of the moon

GRACE

Would you like to come in? Oh god I'm embarrassed! The place is a wreck,
she said to my friend who lowered her hand for the dog to sniff. She
had heard it before, everyone says this, but truly it was. Clothes, toys,
and papers on all available surfaces. Dust, fur and crunchies adrift on
the floor. A sink full of dishes studded with food.

It was a tour of wonderment for my friend, who serves snacks on fine
china, then whisks them away to quickly wash. But she reached for the
baby and gave him a kiss. As the visuals continued, she looked at the
young woman, remarked how, in that moment, the sun through the
window made her hair a halo and glazed the whole kitchen in gold.

> not mother and daughter
> new friends
> no judgment
> kindness sweeps
> the dirty apartment

CLARE DE LUNE

I still have the two figures you made in our ceramics class forty years ago. Each time I moved I discarded stuff, but never the whiskered cat or the gourd-shaped woman.

I'm trying to remember your name. Beautiful and serious, you used to sit calmly with us at the table as we gossiped and laughed, rolling, pounding, shaping clay. Your fingers were magic; a lump of clay within minutes became an animal or person-shaped vessel, shamanistic, seemingly from an ancient time.

Gradually we learned a little about you, unspecified troubles and illnesses, a fragile flower child of a sister, who often waited for you after class. You always put your arm around her.

Many years later I ran into you, still beautiful, thinner, with fine lines all over your pale face. I guessed your troubles had not ebbed, that you had not allowed love into your life, that you lived like a nun — humble, kind, accepting.

I remember your name now: Clare.

> spirit moves through clay
> I sense you
> holding things you made

DAVID, RECENTLY WIDOWED

He sits on the edge of the sofa talking, long stories about little things. He is looking straight into the camera of your eyes. You ask how he's doing. *Listen*, he says. *I'm not sure how I am.* His hands move in air, describing how it is. *I'm lost. It's so quiet, everything.* His eyes and mouth move, afternoon light gentle on his head. You know he will get up and leave as quickly as he came in.

> evening in the armchair
> you think about
> how it must feel
> looking up at stars
> through bare branches

INTERRUPTION

I saw you and although I had a flight to catch and was in mid-conversation, I had to go over and say hello. You were sitting alone on a bleacher, larger than life, curled inward, immobile. I knew as I approached that you would not know me, although we knew each other well. I would have thought you'd know me better now, that omniscience would be the gift death would confer. But you were unconversable, purely interior, stopped as a statue. Nevertheless, I sat down beside you, your absence a presence, the silence a mourning.

co-worker
often we bickered
but once, twice
when I had great need
you soothed me

Driving to LA on 5

Once again I pack my car, pick out cds — Ella singing ballads, Tony duets, the long moody fugues of Alice Coltrane — and coax my dog into the back seat where she will tremble and pant for the first hour. We cross the bridge, glide onto the freeway through the long sprawl of Oakland, past Target, Best Buy, the windmills at Altamont, and ease onto long straight 5 to settle into the road trip.

Vast flat valley, big rigs hurtling, metaphoric cars in queue or maneuvering - Odysseys, Jettas, Mirages, Infinitis — while I, in my Forester, look ahead and around. Not a tree to be found. We stop at a rest stop. *At last!* says my dog. She pulls me along hard clay paths, birds spin from fence post to fence post, rabbits flee into dry golden fields. She sniffs drain pipes in gullies, taking her time. She needs her time.

Many songs, many fugues. I ride into memories, all those people who have been in my life — what was I doing, what was I thinking? Road signs reel off metaphors: Pleasant Valley State Prison, Mercy Hot Springs.

The light turns dark gold on the face of the land, on bare-branched grape vines. We climb the purple mountains of Tejon Pass and descend into the vast pink bowl of LA at twilight, to Pasadena where my mother sits, as always, in her red armchair, a little confused to see me. She seems to be searching for my name. I give her a kiss and ask, *Who am I, Mom? Do you know?*

It takes a minute, she needs a minute. *Of course I do, you're Joyce.*

> landscape gallery
> a tunnel
> leading to you

Beyond Wisdom

Head high, eyes far-visioned, stature propped up with a stick is how she imagined old age — her grandfather's proud pose after his surgery, O'Keefe looking out toward infinite skies.

Even further in life, my mother sits in a wheelchair, mind flickering, wishing for her small bed in the darkened room, knowing perhaps that the slow spiral of days and nights is wrapping around her, and the patient practice of closing one's eyes is moving toward fruition.

> seasons blur
> she recognizes only
> the spoon of oatmeal
> brought to her mouth
> by a familiar face

STOW LAKE

People are at their best at Stow Lake. Couples link arms by the winking water. The dour Russian man, with mutton-chop sideburns, touches his wife's back and points to a hawk circling above. A solitary man is working things out, eyes on the path as he trudges along. Runners like horses glistening with sweat canter round and round the lake, and an old Chinese man at the water's edge meditates, hands on his belly.

In early October, while Blue Angels slashed the sky across town, Eleanor sat and gazed at the lake, the waterfall rushing, the red pavilion, so many birds on the sparkling water. In respite from her illness, she closed her eyes, the sun on her face, and slowly her mind emptied of everything but this: this beautiful, beautiful place.

> out of the water
> onto a rock
> she rests her cheek
> on the warm end
> of summer

Eleanor in the Sun Shining

I wish I could go there, I wish I could stay here, but I am facing The Great Unknown, Eleanor said as we sat in her garden, the sun on our heads, straight shadows of buildings boxing us in. Quaint language, I thought, and murmured something about the months ahead. She sighed, and for a moment out of time, stared into the question that filled her nights, dark space in her mind rolling with stars.

Not without fear, but without dread, Eleanor sat in that small square of sunlight, forwarded to a hospital room where family and friends talked and wept. She listened, not waking, and at midnight when all vastness grew, stepped out like a child into The Great Unknown.

> bright empty square
> shadows of chairs
> a bird singing

Daughters of the Northern Lights, or The Three Suitors: A Tapestry

(Written after viewing the above Norwegian Tapestry, late 1800's.
Gerhard Munthe, designer, Nina Stoltenberg, maker)

Wind has entered the room. The young daughters awaken, startled, disheveled, orange hair in wild flames. One is standing, one rising, one sitting on air or maybe jumping. Their mouths are agape, their eyes blank and glowing.

On the door, a curtain, patterned with loons in flight, has blown open. A blue black sky is studded with stars, or maybe snowflakes suspended. Three white bears have entered, one head up in greeting, one head down covert, one looking straight ahead, their power slung low.

In the near distance, three ducks like boats swim, six ducks like planes plunge down into water. A statue holds an urn of fire. A single dark bird in the midst of a scream hovers over the dream. On the cloth of commotion, the wide-eyed daughters, the advancing bears are suspended in the moment before waking.

> fire of the artist
> a patient woman
> her mind on his dream
> long worked the shuttle,
> tied the knots

Lost in the Woods

Holding her book, dozing, she replied to the dream, *Life is often what we imagine it to be or what it was.* In the netherhood she was a child again, steadfast in the blur, waiting for her parents to come home. She woke on page to know it was not that time. They were not out on errand and back soon, but gone. She was alone as she had been for a long time. The book she was holding was different because as time raced with her, stories came into her hands one by one as they were written.

> library of time
> a curious child
> wanders
> into giant forests
> of adult literature

TRANSPORT

I read so many novels and watch so many movies, I get confused. Who was the woman not in love with that perfect man who loved her all his life? Didn't he play the stalker in another movie? What were their names anyway, and what happened in the end? I seem to recall some small tragic mistake.

I never confuse those lives with my own which I plan daily for a regimen of exercise, entertainment, getting together with friends, and a little creativity.

If not for those novels and films and songs that play over and over in my head, and friends and sisters who involve me occasionally in emotional turmoil, I wonder where's the excitement in my life at this time? It's been a while since I've wanted a lover, but I do wish for another friend like Anne, who pulled me into moments she enjoyed like a child.

She was like a novel, a film, a song.

> a teenager reads
> *Gone with the Wind*
> dramatic possibilities
> her life begins
> to open

Hotel New Wave

I study my clothes at the Hotel New Wave. What to wear? Putting on the trenchcoat of my younger self, I listen. The evening begins to form a dialogue.

The hallways are filled with people I knew, who changed my life with a look or touch. In passing, I ask each one, *Where will you be next?* — as if we could plan to meet again. An unaccompanied cello plays as I clatter down stairs into the illumination of a Paris night. Or did that happen in a Truffault film?

She looks away from the man she has long watched. He lights her cigarette. The room fills with desire.

> black high heels clicking
> on lamplit sidewalks
> a nightbook of stories
> the unhappy mouth
> of Jeanne Moreau

Animus

After all these years in another country, I meet an old sweetheart and wonder if our feelings could be the same. We kiss, and I think...*It could happen again.*

He takes me to his childhood home, a tiny house with so many people, his father, his brothers. The father is bitter and orders my sweetheart to put his World War II souvenirs on the wall. *Which one will you buy?* he asks me. *It's for the vets.*

The souvenirs are old and handmade: a Japanese handkerchief printed with stars and a cross, blue paper posters crackled with age, a piece of wire encased in cloth.

I turn to my sweetheart and see he is still in thrall to that little house, to that angry father, and know he will never, ever be mine.

> souls come back
> to live again
> I know this place...you
> and again
> stars are falling

Bon Voyage

Sometimes, to keep energy spinning, we wrap up everyone we've ever been and take ourselves to a place or person or glimmering idea — a new beginning where we continue our soliloquies, dialogues, diatribes and sonnets.

The Hindus say all is illusion, that after acts of conflict from the troubled mind, speech from the complex heart, the play will be over. We will take our bows, and our lives will spin into transparency.

But we are not there yet, there is much to do. We unpack ourselves like beasts of burden, leaving behind as much as we can, to sense the air when the dream turns around to face us.

> interiors shine
> she passes by
> lit windows
> places where
> she no longer lives

LAST VISIT AT THE NURSING HOME

Reclining in that complicated wheelchair, the tiny hull of her body lay light as an insect cradled on a leaf. Her eyes are bright when she doesn't drift to sleep in little puffs of exhaustion. Someone has painted her fingernails a robin's egg blue. Her old self would have been appalled, but now she seems to like them. Her hair is not the way she would have liked — neatly styled. A strand is close to her eye, and the back of her head mussed. All those naps. I brush the hair away from her face.

Our aunt had been a smart, vibrant woman, happy to keep a clean house, fixing huge meals every day for her family, talking and listening to anyone who came by with news or a problem, singing in the church choir, speaking her mind in the community about issues important to her.

At times in the past two years, she would converse spiritedly into the wild blue yonder. Now, she is so tired she can barely speak. We lean in to listen when she opens her mouth; her eyelids tremble. "You're here. I'm glad."

> then we realize
> we are all butterflies
> loss in the air

The Calligraphy of Mimi

The lines of living are established, radiate around centers of activity: the mouth and eyes. Laughter and pleasure have made their marks. Finer lines on the forehead, between the brows, show tracery of worry. Her calligraphic mouth registers thought with a slight change in the curve. Under dark wings of her brows, her eyes seek out everything, the smallest detail, the huge expanse.

When we went to China, as our boat navigated the high narrow gorges of the Yangtze, I stood in the crowded dry cabin watching Mimi on deck in what was sometimes hard rain, sometimes drenching mist, her two dollar poncho streaming. She had pulled a chair to the front tip of the boat, gazed out and around, determined to miss not a thing.

> she can talk your ear off
> yet her hand
> draws quiet grace
> the line of a wave
> almost touching the beach

HONEYMOON SNAPSHOT, 1959

She is stepping around the car towards him, grinning, knowing he is about to perform a little prank just for her. The photo seems like part of a movie we're all watching and enjoying, a stop somewhere in the vast U.S.A., the borrowed convertible parked and plump. He is sly and masterful, will pull this one off, whatever it is. She'll clap and laugh but won't remember in this favorite photo what he was doing. So many funny things he pulled from the air for her eternal delight.

> *before I was born*
> the child muses
> seeing
> her mother and father
> at play

DANNY IN BROOKLYN

He was a delightful and skilled lover of women. Not long after he started at her toes, working his way up to her laughing face, he broke her heart. She was very young and grieved fiercely. After five decades and a long love marriage, the memory of Danny could still bring her joy and pain.

A few years after her husband died, she searched and found him. They talked on the phone, exchanged photos. He: your hair is gray! She: and where is yours? Fascinated but wary he came to San Francisco, walked the city for hours before knocking on her door.

After a few charmed days, he stole away without a goodbye. She thought regretfully that he wasn't so different, although she was wiser. And as before, she hadn't the chance to wish him love.

> red geraniams spill
> over a retaining wall
> late Brooklyn afternoons

MY DATE WITH HUGH

Somehow, wherever I was, I found myself with Hugh Grant. He was in a room nearby, a little sick or injured, and somewhat bored and whiny. I brought him a cup of tea for which he was grateful, and happy when I agreed to go for a ride.

He had a big blue convertible which was very old. As we rode through Malibu with the top down, I was surprised no one recognized him, even though he didn't look his best.

We drove to an ocean overlook and started to go down a rocky narrow road. But after a few feet, I said, "No, back up — this is not safe for an old blue convertible". We went to the beach instead and walked, enjoying the blue breezy air.

I am puzzled. Although entranced by your tics and stumbles, I was never in love with you. What were you doing in my dream, Hugh?

> the people
> you don't meet
> except in dreams
> familiar
> as family

The Art of Conversation

In the first light moments of her widowhood, open to catching some-one's sparkle and kindness, she would chat up strangers at the bus stop. She'd tell a joke; they would laugh and talk; and when they parted to board, would sometimes call out, "You're so nice! Will you marry me?"

They would grin and wave, flashing on her sparkle and kindness, and maybe the loneliness. When the moment ended, she was reminded it was just her solo in the world, making new and necessary connections through the circle of days, inviting friends to her sonorous house to sit over tea at the kitchen table. She would laugh and talk, smoothing out like a cloth, the fine details of the past, the moment, and the blurred and varied outlines of what was yet to come.

> I told her one day
> I would channel her
> and with a lighthearted joke
> begin
> all encounters

SPIRIT HORSE

Each time I visited, Anne would fix me a cup of tea and show me something from her past. One day, it was a photo her late husband took of a white horse at twilight. Its head was ghostly, the beautiful strong haunches blurred in slow canter, the meadows darkening.

Spirit Horse, she said, her eyes filling with tears. Because I admired it, she gave me a copy, a memento of her beloved, whom I never knew.

Now, she too is gone, away to the ethers. I look at the photo on this gray day and imagine souls softly moving in waning pink light.

> bright sun
> shadow of her hands
> holding a cup of tea

What She Was Thinking

She treasured her body, was organic vegetarian, but relented a little when she dined with friends. She strived to live well, with love, with thought. After the news she said, *I wonder when I can no longer sit in the kitchen with you, or climb the stairs to my bed.*

Still with friends she would listen and talk. One by one, we sat on the sofa as she reclined, her feet on our lap. Sometimes, it seemed no different from before; we said whatever came to mind. It was always that way with her, but now with more intent; the illness was moving as fast as a river.

When she tired, she asked us to read to her, the Endpoint poems of John Updike, the dark grieving journeys of W.G. Sebald. She had always loved great tragic books, chronicles of pain and death. Her eyes darkened as she listened. When we stopped, she looked out the window, at rustling trees across the street, rooted houses on the hill, and asked us the question she was asking herself.

What do you think about what's happening to me?

> painting with water
> on white parchment
> the unsayable

SKY

She floats on her back in the middle of a lake. Her mind is clear and open. She wonders if this will ever happen again, being gently centered with the sky arching above.

In the house where she has lived more than half her life, she lies on the sofa, floats on the raft of a pill. Her eyes drift over the books and flowers on the coffee table, mementos and photos on the mantel, paintings and her husband's photographs on the wall. Friends had asked her, *Is that nude of you?* and she always answered, *Of course it is*, although it isn't.

The sun moves along the warm wall. They had fought over its color, and she speaks again to the dear departed. *Yes, you were right, my love. This soft grey is exactly right.* Remembering him, she falls asleep.

And wakes to find that change has occurred. A different sofa, different art — spare, colorful, modern. Young voices call to one another, footsteps move from room to room, new layers accrue on walls, on surfaces. She looks around in admiration; the house resonates with the future. She leaves.

We will remember this immense sky until we die.

> dear friend
> the flowers, the trees
> admired on our walks
> neighborhood the same
> remembering you

Qi Gong Class at Aquatic Park Senior Center

Dark afternoon. Winter has come. Somehow we have made our way here against our will, with a weak blind faith it will make things better. Our teacher, gentlest man, leads us in Wild Goose — moving arms slowly in wide dipping arcs — until, he says, we merge with the universe.

None of us has ever done that, although he believes we will. Through tall windows we see black blooming clouds, pelicans gliding, and a single swimmer stroking smoothly across the cove, as if it were natural to be courageous. He or she must know how to merge.

We continue to move in long repetitions, remember Anne who was here last winter and died in the spring, who would have taken in with us the darkness of this afternoon.

> the sky so dramatic
> simultaneous
> our grieving

INTO THE NIGHT

She was an old dog. I was expecting it, or so I told myself.

On her last day, we took slow walks. She sniffed her favorite places thoroughly, peed and pooped, loved her breakfast and dinner.

The evening was terrifying and fast. Suddenly she was careening around the room, her legs wild and weak, and collapsed. She began to cry and cry, sounds she had never made before, and banged her head against the floor. Then the long ride through cool dark streets to the 24 hour vet.

        on this night
        of her death
        I think I hear her
        shift weight
        in the dark

Lost Dog

It was a fantastic place for dogs: soft green hills, graceful old trees, flowery meadows in gentle light. And not far from home — why hadn't I known about this? I watched in amazement as a man on a horse, leading another black horse, sailed over a valley through an endless blue sky. Bold, confident, they landed solidly and galloped away. Then, all these dogs, like great birds in flight, made the same leap.

I looked around for my dog; she wasn't on leash. I thought I saw her at the top of a ridge and called to her. She raced down and sat in front of me, panting, waiting for her treat. But it wasn't her. I walked the trails, calling and calling. It was getting dark.

I took off my shoes and put my socks at a crossroad of many paths, so she'd know to wait for me there. Ragtag clouds were fiery; the sun dropped into the ocean. As I walked back to the car, darkness within me grew as I repeated, *I'm lost, I'm lost, I'm lost.*

in this empty house
my love for you
flows everywhere

As It Is On Earth

My friend Nancy says that every time she lost a dog, she was assured either by a voice or dream that her dog was in safe hands. "We've got her," a voice told her, as she walked home from the vet after putting Ginger down. Wendy believes she will be surrounded by all her past dogs and cats in a place something like heaven when she dies.

I believe Cori is gone, except in my mind, just as I will be gone, except in the minds of those who knew me. For a while though, her passing made me wonder, more than the death of any person, about an afterlife. "Where did she go?" I found myself asking those first few days.

I don't think about that anymore, but her death does make me wonder what breezes of joy, alleys of grief await me in the years to come.

> dog heaven
> nosing into fragrant grasses
> trotting along in fine blue air
> the human humming along
> dog heart full

Cats and Dogs

On the first night of our visit, after we devoured the hot rice and cold sashimi she fixed, my best friend and I argued twice — first about cats, second about dogs.

I said it would be a while before I'd get another dog, but I missed an animal presence in my house. Maybe I would get a cat, one who would be happy indoors. The outdoors worried me — cars, coyotes, bird killing, viruses. She, mother of neighborhood feral cats, said that would be cruel; a cat needed to roam outside to be happy. We agreed to stop talking about it after a heated 15 minutes.

Then we talked about a neighbor who probably fed her French pug to death. Toward the end, he was so obese he couldn't walk. I would see her pull him down the sidewalk in a cushioned red wagon, an immense toad prince melting into folds of himself. My friend was outraged — people like that shouldn't have pets. I said I thought that too at first, but the old woman and her dog adored each other. She said it was abuse; I said it was just another case of imperfect love in the world. We couldn't agree on a single thing that night.

> birds on a wire
> in our empathic youth
> the topic was men

GRIEF

To be flat and dark as a shadow, reflecting shapes of vibrant things
— flowers in a vase, a shimmering elm, sphinx of a dog basking — is
comforting. On my walks I stop and look at the drift of shadows on
the sidewalk. Sometimes, I squint beyond and see huge cloud shadows
on the gray green mountains. That they move so slowly is reassuring to
me. These days I go to quietude as I lay on the sofa thinking nothing,
seeing the soft shapes of things around the room. White curtains spin
a fine transparent darkness onto the floor.

> bright moon
> my long shadow
> begins to climb
> out of the half existence
> of loss

METAMORPHOSIS

I learned from my dog what wildness is. I remember her young self running through meadows of purple ice plants by the ocean, pouncing on mice like an arctic wolf, racing up and down hills, crisscrossing trails. Only occasionally in these solitary celebrations would she circle back from a distance to see where I was. Eventually, she'd return to me, happily panting.

As she grew old and slow, she became more a house pet. My once aloof-as-a-cat dog became openly affectionate, following me around, pressing her forehead to my knee in a pure declaration of love. I took for granted our simple relationship, how we could say with a glance: *Time for a walk? A treat? What do you need? To be with you.*

She was such a quiet dog, I'd forget she was there. Now, I hear a soft sound and think she's in another room.

> spring of white blossoms
> the grieving mother
> bids farewell

MAN WITH COCKATOO

If I were dreaming, I would talk to the man who often walks up my street with a white cockatoo on his leather-bound arm. The man looks ascetic, small and lean, a bit like my father in an alternate universe, without wife or children. I've never tried to speak to him, and he never acknowledges me and my dog. But I understand. How can he think of anything but what he carries, that solid magical idol of snowy purity? And what could I say to such a pair? Do I have questions for which I need answers?

But in the world that is my dream, I say "Blessings, dear shaman, homage to your bird!" and watch him turn onto mythic streets, pixelating into stars.

> stranger
> you say
> there are many ways
> to simply love
> in this multifarious world

ABOUT THE AUTHOR

J oyce Futa has been living in Altadena, California for the past four years, after living in San Francisco for 50 years. She has been happy to find a wonderful community of poets there. *Lit Windows: A Book of Haibun and Tanka Prose* is her first book of poetry.

www.ingramcontent.com/pod-product-compliance
Lightning Source LLC
Chambersburg PA
CBHW032034090426
42741CB00006B/809